Performers in Uniform

THE THUNDERBIRDS

By Peter B. Mohn

Photographs courtesy of
the U.S. Air Force

Consultant:
James C. Jannette, Captain, U.S.A.F.
Public Affairs Officer, Thunderbirds

CHILDRENS PRESS, CHICAGO

ACKNOWLEDGEMENTS

Special thanks to a number of Thunderbirds I've known and met since 1975. Particular thanks
to Captain Bob Gore, Major Chris Patterakis and to Major D.L. Smith and the 1979 Thunderbirds.

Library of Congress Cataloging in Publication Data

Mohn, Peter B
  The Thunderbirds.

  (Performers in uniform)
  SUMMARY: Describes the operation of the Thunderbirds
of the U.S. Air Force, including the team's history,
selection and training of personnel, aircraft maintenance,
and planning and executing a show.
  1. United States. Air Force. 4520th Aerial
Demonstration Team—Juvenile literature. [1. United
States. Air Force. 4520th Aerial Demonstration Team.
2. Stunt flying. 3. Aeronautics, Military] I. Title.
UG633-M54   797.5'4   79-25914
·ISBN 0-516-01954-6

SURPRISE!

Where were the Thunderbirds?

The large crowd had seen the six planes take off a few minutes before. Now, however, the only Thunderbird they could see was Captain Jim Jiggens, the narrator, who stood in front of them.

As Captain Jiggens talked about the history of the United States Air Force team, many people looked toward the sky. They looked left and right. They looked up. But all they saw was the sky and a few thin clouds.

Where were the Thunderbirds?

Captain Jiggens told the crowd that the team was first organized in 1953 at Luke Air Force Base in Arizona. He said that the team had flown for people in 45 foreign countries.

One by one, he introduced the Thunderbirds' ground crew. Captain Jiggens told the crowd that in 26 years, the Thunderbirds had not missed a show because an aircraft wasn't ready.

Still, the crowd had come to see the Thunderbirds fly and they hadn't seen anything yet. More and more people began to look around.

Captain Jiggens described the team's training. He told how the Thunderbirds practiced twice a day during the winter months at Nellis Air Force Base near Las Vegas, Nevada.

Down the flight line near the trailer, Major Fred Erickson, the Number Seven Thunderbird, turned toward the crowd. He wore headphones with a microphone attached to them.

"Roger," he said into the microphone, then he turned to a group of ground crew.

"They're coming in," he said.

The crowd heard the Thunderbirds first. The roar of eight jet engines in the four planes swept over them. Then coming from behind the crowd, the Thunderbirds shot by at 500 miles per hour. They pulled up into a graceful formation loop. Their smoke trails lingered over the crowd.

The show had begun.

"We almost always begin our shows from behind the crowd," said one Thunderbird, laughing. "We get their attention that way."

TWICE A DAY

"I thought I flew a lot before I joined the Thunderbirds," said a Thunderbird pilot. "But when you're a member of this team, that's when you fly a lot."

The team usually starts putting its show together in December. That's when three new pilots join, and they have to learn how to fly in tight formations and do the maneuvers.

"The training isn't difficult," a pilot said. "It's very different, though. We are doing many of the same things we did while flying jet fighter planes. The difference is that the Thunderbirds fly much closer together."

Most Air Force pilots have flown the Thunderbirds' T-38A "Talon." It is the aircraft used to train most people who go on to flying fighter aircraft.

"We start out flying in two-plane formations in December," explained Captain Ron Maness, the left wingman. Captain Maness keeps track of the training flights. "The first two-plane flights take place over a dry lake not far from Nellis."

"In the first few weeks, the training takes place fairly high in the sky," added the right wingman, Captain Jim Latham. "The two aircraft get into most of the aerobatics done by the whole team."

"Two things begin to happen in these flights," Captain Maness said. "The pilots begin to get a feel for flying close together, and they start to develop confidence in the other pilots."

When all the pilots have finished their two-plane flights, the Thunderbirds put their diamond formation together. The practice goes on, twice a day.

"When the diamond comes together, the load shifts to the shoulders of the Boss," said a Thunderbird. "We all follow his lead and keep station on his plane. Wherever he goes or whatever he does, we follow."

Number One, the Boss, talks to the other aircraft by radio.

"He keeps us informed," said Major Jim Coziahr, slot pilot. "If the Boss changes his speed, he tells us. If he's going to pull up or turn or roll, we know before he does it. We're using our controls almost all the time, too."

After every flight, whether two-plane or diamond, there's a debriefing. The pilots go to the conference room in the Thunderbird hangar and review their flight.

"Our debriefings are closed to everyone but the pilots," said Major D. L. Smith, Thunderbird leader. "If something was done wrong, we talk about it. Sometimes we really let our hair down."

"The first debriefing I saw was really rough," said a Thunderbird. "One of the pilots got onto another for something he did wrong. But the other guy just admitted that he'd been off a little and asked how to correct it."

More Thunderbird crew members get involved when the formation flights shift to Indian Springs, an auxiliary airfield about 50 miles from Nellis.

Major Fred Erickson, the team's logistics and safety officer, follows the formation through its maneuvers in the Number Seven aircraft. A technician makes a videotape of every practice.

"By late winter we have most of our show put together," Major Smith said. "Our practices are used to knock off the rough edges. Once our season begins, our practice flights are called 'rough edges' drills. We may do one maneuver several times in a row to be sure we have it right."

Being able to videotape the practices and the shows has given the team a much better picture of itself, one Thunderbird said.

"The tapes don't lie. If someone has been a little out of position, or if he's late in making a move, the tape will show it. I've flown any number of maneuvers and thought I was perfect, only to have the tape show me I was off."

"Most people in the crowd don't see our shows as we do," Major Smith added. "We are always looking for total perfection, and we keep on working toward it in every show or practice session."

The new Thunderbirds learn quickly to accept criticism, and to criticize others. "Even before I joined the team I knew that the debriefings would be tough at times," said a pilot.

Even the candidates for the team take part in the debriefings, Captain Maness said. From what they notice, and what they say during the debriefings, "We can get a pretty good picture of what kind of Thunderbird each one will make."

For many years, the Thunderbirds flew with five aircraft and just one solo pilot. In 1979 they added a second solo plane and Captain R.D. Evans flew it.

"It was a very interesting year," said Captain Gail "Scar" Scarbrough, the lead solo pilot, who was in his second year with the team. "R.D. and I sort of had to put a whole new act together. Then we had to polish it. It was a good experience."

The solo aircraft fly "opposing" maneuvers in which they fly at one another at speeds near 500 miles per hour. They fly together at other times, and for a handful of maneuvers they fly with the diamond aircraft.

"We debrief our own maneuvers," Captain Scarbrough said, "But we also take part in the discussion of the maneuvers that we fly with the diamond."

"There's a very good reason for going after perfection in what we do," said Major Smith. "If we do our flying perfectly, we know we'll be perfectly safe."

NEVER A MISS

By the end of 1978, the Thunderbirds had flown more than 2,200 air shows. They hadn't missed a single show in any type of aircraft because a plane wasn't ready to fly.

"The credit for that record belongs to our non-commissioned officers," said Major Smith. "I don't think there's a group of men and women who work harder anywhere in the armed forces."

The 70 or so non-commissioned officers in the team go to work early in the day. They will work until late at night if they have to. As many as thirty of them may travel with the team during the show season.

"We have at least one specialist in every area we need to keep the planes in the air," said Staff Sergeant Todd Flannery, crew chief for the Number Two Thunderbird in 1979. "Sometimes you'll see almost everyone working on one or two of the planes if they have problems and a flight is going out soon."

When the Thunderbirds are home at Nellis Air Force
Base, the planes are kept in a hangar with a shiny gray floor
and the team's insignia painted on it.

"The longer we use the planes we have, the greater our
problems become," said Major Erickson, who's also in
charge of maintenance. "Aircraft get old too, and we've
been flying these T-38As for five years."

When a pilot finds that something is wrong with his
aircraft, he gives his crew chief a written report. It's the
crew chief's job to correct the problem.

"Sometimes you can go for two or three weeks without a
single 'write-up,'" Sergeant Flannery said. "Then in one
week, you can get one or two a day."

The crew chief usually begins the repair, according to Flannery. If he needs help from one of the specialists, he asks for it.

"All of the aircraft have to go through regular inspections," he added. "We go through each one very carefully. We look for cracks in the structures. We check each system in the planes. If anything isn't 100 per cent, it gets fixed.

"The major inspections are usually done during the winter. That's when the aircraft are torn down and *really* checked out. It takes quite a bit more time to do the annual inspection."

As Flannery spoke, the loudspeakers in the Thunderbird hangar spoke. "Boat-tail call. Number eight," they said.

"Back to work," Flannery said. "The boat-tail is the rear part of the plane. The 'stabilator' comes off in one piece, and it has to be removed to do engine work. The boat-tail is big and heavy, so no one runs away from a boat-tail call."

Almost a dozen Thunderbirds helped to lift the boat-tail into place and slide it over the two jet engines. Then, when it was in place, several crew members held it there with their backs while others bolted it in.

"With the Thunderbirds you never work alone," said Staff Sergeant Fred Simione, Number One crew chief. "There's always someone available to help if you need it."

"We try to do most of our heavy work at home," said Major Erickson. "It isn't always possible, though. We have had to make engine changes while traveling, and other major problems have come up.

"We have the Number Seven and Eight aircraft for backup, which helps, but mostly we have the ground crew. I think they can do almost everything."

One of the crew chiefs flies with his plane to the show sites. The pilot's name is printed in white letters on both sides of the aircraft. The name of one crew member is on one side, the other chief's name is on the other.

"That's one of the bonuses," said Sergeant Flannery. "When you get to travel in the aircraft you take care of you really feel like you've done something good. The other thing is when they do an arrival demonstration."

When coming into a show site, the Thunderbirds usually put on a 10 to 15 minute show. "This has given me a real feeling for what the plane and the pilot go through during a regular show," Flannery said.

Many people think that the only Thunderbirds are the pilots, and that the ground crew are just people who follow them, according to Flannery.

1979 Thunderbird non-commissioned officers, front row, l to r, CMSgt. "Heggy" Heggerston, MSgt Jerry Petrick, SSgt Colin Jenkins, SSgt Dave Branks, SSgt John Rabba, SSgt Charlie Urbano, SSgt Larry Burlingame, SrA Beth Coffua, SSgt Gary Holland, SSgt Jimmy Steele, MSgt Jack Abrams, SSgt Pat Smith, TSgt Ron VanAlstine, SSgt Marc Cargo and MSgt Denny Philebar. **Second row,** l to r, SSgt Delores Lillard, SSgt Mike Cook, TSgt Chuck Langgin, SSgt Huey Helms, SSgt Enrico Calabrese, Sgt Bob Ulman, TSgt Brock McMahon, SSgt Ray Osborn, SSgt Dean Coker, SSgt Bob McCall, MSgt Phil Summers, SSgt Carl Priddy, SMSgt Larry Helmerick and SSgt Ramon Badia. **Third row,** l to r, Sgt Bryan Clark, Sgt Don Tisdale, MSgt Ken McGlothlin, SSgt Wayne Johnson, TSgt Pat Prim, SSgt Steve Goshe, SSgt Frank Kelly, SSgt Tommy Sims, SSgt Dave Thrower, TSgt Rick Heinrichs, TSgt Roy Miller, SSgt Todd Flannery, TSgt Dave Shackelford and SSgt Fred Simione. **Top row,** l to r, SSgt Pat Wright, MSgt Earl Godby, SSgt Jim Brohn, SSgt Brian Gilbert, TSgt Buster Helms, TSgt Mike Cleveland, SSgt Jim Wiley, SSgt Jerry Holland, MSgt Paul Fisher, SSgt Bill Powers, SSgt Tom Brick, TSgt Tom Jones, TSgt Dave Warren, TSgt Buster LaGarde and TSgt Jerry Imada.

"We're all Thunderbirds too," he said. "We have to volunteer for the team and go through a selection process just like the pilots. We sign up for a two-year term like the pilots. We can, if we want, ask for a third year."

The Thunderbird ground crewmen and women also look at many applications before they choose their people.

"We're as picky as the pilots," one of them said. "And if you see someone around here who's not wearing the Thunderbird patch on his or her shirt, that's because he or she is on probation.

"For 30 days after people go to work here, we watch them carefully. If they fit in and do their jobs well, they earn their Thunderbird patch. If they don't, they may go back to their old unit."

Many of the Thunderbird ground crew have families who live near or on the base. Flannery said the families ought to be Thunderbirds too.

"They go through a lot for us," he said. "We work long hours. Then we're gone sometimes for two or three weeks at a time, come home for a day or two, and then go again.

"You know? Just about the time I leave on a trip is when the kids get sick, the car breaks down, or the dog bites somebody. My family has to handle trouble without me."

CHOOSING THE THUNDERBIRDS

"We are as careful about choosing new people as we are about flying our aircraft," said Major Coziahr, whose job it is to handle new officer applications for the team.

"These new pilots are going to make maybe 500 practice and show flights in their two years. They have to work together. They must get along well, fly well, and meet the people well."

Coziahr makes sure that each of the Thunderbird officers reads all the applications. A sheet on each application carries comments from every officer.

"We get the applications in the spring," Coziahr said. "Each one shows what the applicant has done during his career. There are notes about him from his commanding officers. We ask him to tell us why he wants to be a Thunderbird.

"After we've looked at every applicant, we choose around 15 men. They are invited to join us on one show trip, and they spend a few days with the team. After we have seen each of these semi-finalists, we cut the list to six."

The semi-finalists do more than watch the team in action. They sit in on briefings and debriefings. They are asked to comment on the shows and practices. All that time, the eyes and ears of the men on the team are wide open.

Late in the summer, the six pilots—now finalists—go to Nellis Air Force Base. This time, they fly in the back seats of the T-38As. The Thunderbird in the front seat puts the finalist through a very exacting check flight.

1979 Thunderbird officers, front row, l to r, Major D. L. Smith, commander/leader, Rossville, GA; left wing, Captain Ron Maness, Carthage, NC; right wing, Captain Jim Latham, Shawnee Mission, KS; slot, Captain Jim Coziahr, Orion, IL; lead solo, Captain Gail "Scar" Scarbrough, Grover Hill, OH; second solo, Captain R. D. Evans, Osceola, AR; logistics officer, Major Fred Erickson, Albany, GA; and narrator, Captain Jim Jiggens, Northville, MI. **Top row,** l to r, executive officer, Major Steve Hyle, Lancaster, OH; chief of maintenance, Captain Bob Biehl, Marion, IN and public affairs, Captain Jim Jannette, Mentor, OH. (U.S. Air Force Photo)

"In a way I guess we put these guys through the wringer," said Captain Maness. "By the time we're done, though, we know exactly what kind of pilots they are and what kind of people they are."

"Deciding who's to join and who isn't is hard," Major Coziahr added. "Those six finalists are almost always top-flight men."

When the fall comes, the Thunderbird pilots meet once more to talk about the six men. When the meeting is over, three of the six will be Thunderbirds the next year.

Every other year, the team must choose the man to be its Boss for the next two years.

"The team leader is the most important man," said Captain Maness, "and it's only right that he be chosen by members of the team. We may be the only group of our kind to choose our leaders."

The men who want to lead the Thunderbirds are checked out in the same way as the other pilots. Four men in Thunderbird history have been chosen twice—once as a formation or solo pilot, the second time as Number One.

There are more people to be chosen than just for the aircraft. Among the officers, the Thunderbirds have a maintenance officer, who oversees the repairing and upkeep on the planes. The executive officer represents the Number One Thunderbird when the team is away, and the public affairs officer takes care of the publicity.

Among the non-commissioned officers there also are specialists in photography, art, administration, and publicity.

"THUNDERBIRDS...NOW"

The pilots were dressed in white flight suits and red jackets; the ground crewmen in blue uniforms. The show was to go on in 15 minutes. They stood around the Thunderbirds' sound and radio trailer, talking.

One by one, the crew chiefs found their pilots, came to attention and saluted. After the pilot returned the salute, they shook hands smartly and relaxed. Captain Jiggens looked over his book for the narration while Major Erickson put on his headphones.

Three men who wanted to be Thunderbirds also were there. They, too, wore headphones so they could hear the radio talk between the pilots.

The first Thunderbirds to march out to the flight line were the crew chiefs and the line chief. They marched in formation down the line with each plane's crew dropping out as they got to their aircraft.

Next came the six pilots, Major Smith in the lead. They marched down the flight line in the same way the crews had. Each was saluted by his crew. Then the pilots walked out in front of their aircraft and stood facing them.

"Let's go!" yelled Major Smith. With that, he and the five other pilots ran quickly to their aircraft and all but flew into the cockpits. Quickly they put on their seat harnesses and helmets with help from a ground crewman. When all were harnessed and helmeted, they began to crank their engines.

When all engines were started and preflight checks finished, the roaring aircraft taxied to the runway. The four diamond planes were first to take off and they were followed quickly by the solo pilots.

The Thunderbirds' first pass over the field came from behind the crowd. It surprised many of the people. Major Smith led his team through a loop, pulling over the top at about 6,500 feet above the ground. Next, it was the solo pilots' turn. They flashed through the show area, rolling their aircraft 90 degrees to vertical as they passed.

During the show Major Smith and Captain Scarbrough do most of the talking on the radio.

"The Boss (Major Smith) lets us know what he's doing at all times," Captain Maness said. "If he changes speed just a little bit or a lot, or if he's starting a maneuver, he calls it."

Major Smith speaks with an even voice.

"Coming up . . . 400 (miles per hour) . . . Thunderbirds, right turn . . . now!" The other three pilots in the formation position their aircraft around Number One. Each keeps his eyes on the Boss. Each tries to keep in exactly the same position on his wing.

"It gets a little tough some times," said Captain Maness. "We fly in an awful lot of bumpy air, and that can cause problems. The big thing, though, is that we trust the Boss, and each other. He won't get us into trouble, and we know it."

"In the solo routine we have different problems," said Captain Scarbrough. "Wind is one of the biggest ones.

"Every 10 knots (or miles per hour) of wind will make a one-second difference in our speed down the show line. Captain Evans and I want to make all our crosses exactly at the center point. If the wind is blowing down the show line, the pilot flying into it will have to start a little earlier."

The Thunderbirds fly a "high" show in clear weather and a "low" show when it's overcast.

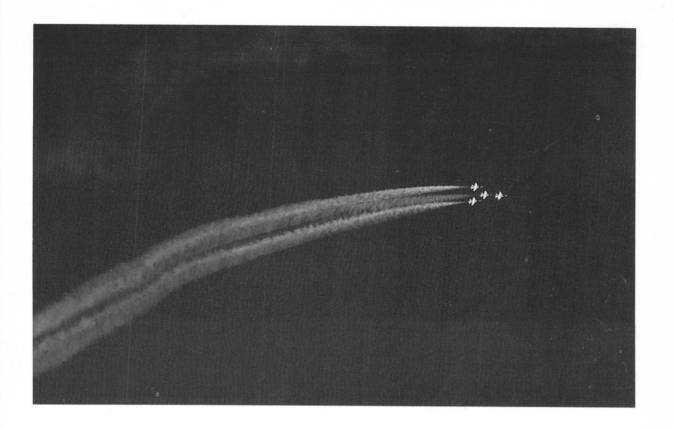

"We always want to give our crowds the full show with the vertical high climbs," said Major Smith. "But we can almost always give them a good show if we have 2,500 or so feet of clear air above the show site."

Perhaps the most spectacular of the team's maneuvers is the bomb burst. In it, the diamond planes are followed by one solo pilot into a vertical, maximum performance climb.

As they climb, they begin to slow down a little. At the top of their climb, Major Smith calls for a break. The four diamond planes break out of formation and each goes a different direction. The solo pilot keeps on going up— straight up—rolling his aircraft as he does.

"I think the rollback is one of the best of the rolling maneuvers," Captain Latham said. "In it, the two wingmen roll out of the diamond. Then we roll right back in only we're on the wings of the slot man instead of the leader."

Captain Maness said the team often has problems with bumpy air. "Some days we must get it pretty well stirred up. But all four planes hit the same bumps at about the same time. This makes you work much harder to keep the formation."

"I don't think our crowds see us hit the bumps," a Thunderbird added. "To the people watching it looks pretty smooth. Sometimes, though, the aircraft are bobbing around like corks in rough water. Flying in bumpy air is much more tiring because you're always correcting for the bumps."

"I like to listen to the crowd during the shows," said one ground crewman. "The different maneuvers make the crowd really respond.

"They seem to like the simple stuff too. When Captain Evans comes in flying very slowly and Captain Scarbrough passes him at 650 miles an hour it really gets them going."

THUNDERBIRD MANEUVERS

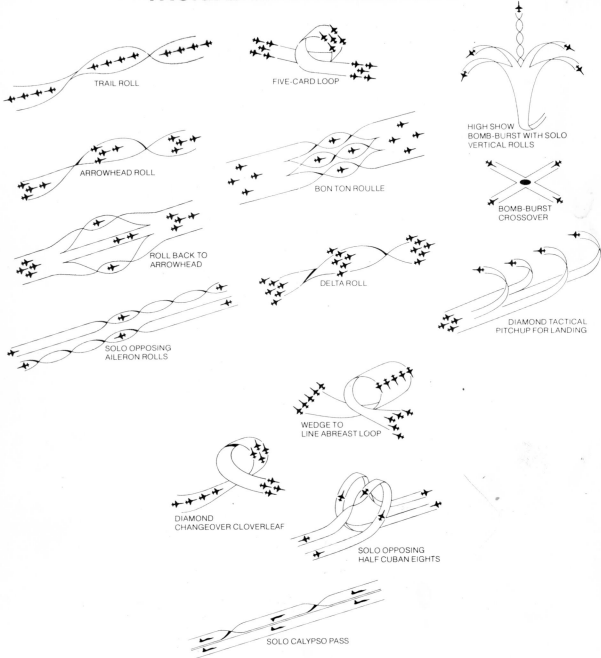

TRAIL ROLL

FIVE-CARD LOOP

HIGH SHOW
BOMB-BURST WITH SOLO
VERTICAL ROLLS

ARROWHEAD ROLL

BON TON ROULLE

BOMB-BURST
CROSSOVER

ROLL BACK TO
ARROWHEAD

DELTA ROLL

DIAMOND TACTICAL
PITCHUP FOR LANDING

SOLO OPPOSING
AILERON ROLLS

WEDGE TO
LINE ABREAST LOOP

DIAMOND
CHANGEOVER CLOVERLEAF

SOLO OPPOSING
HALF CUBAN EIGHTS

SOLO CALYPSO PASS

One of the main rolling maneuvers is called the "Bon Ton Roulle," and that, according to Captain Jiggens, means, "Let the Good Times Roll." The aircraft come down the show line in a loose diamond formation. On signal from the leader, each plane does a quick roll.

At 430 miles per hour, the roll takes very little time. The leader and right wingman do their rolls to the right; left wingman and slot pilot to the left.

"I kind of like the chance I get to do high performance aileron rolls," said Captain Scarbrough. "I come down the line at almost 500 miles per hour and start rolling. No, I don't get dizzy."

"What we're showing is the ability of the Air Force," said Captain Evans. "Everything that we do might be useful if we have to fly in combat against other aircraft. All Air Force pilots are trained to fly as we do, and will be trained like that in the years to come."

WARRIORS AT PEACE

Most Thunderbird pilots have been in combat. The earliest Thunderbirds were veterans of World War II. Later team members flew over Korea and Vietnam.

"A man doesn't have to have combat experience to join this team," said Major Smith. "It happens, however, that most of us have been to war. By the mid-eighties, if there are no more actions, maybe none of the Thunderbirds will have combat behind them."

"It's even possible that we may have women Thunderbird pilots in the early or mid-eighties," Smith added. "We have women instructors in the T-38 now. They don't have the 1,000 hours of flight time we require. But by 1981 or 1982, some will."

A person wanting to become an Air Force pilot must graduate from college. After joining the Air Force, he or she gets more than a year of flight training. They can choose between flying jet fighters, bombers, helicopters, or transport aircraft.

Most of the Thunderbirds have been interested in flying since they were young.

"I can't remember a day since my childhood when I didn't want to fly," said Major Smith, whose father also was in the Air Force.

Captain Scarbrough was drawn into the Air Force by seeing a Thunderbird show when he was younger.

"The show was an experience I never forgot," he said years later. "It made me more determined to graduate from college and become an Air Force pilot."

Major Coziahr spent his first few years in the Air Force as an enlisted man.

"I started out as a sheet metal man, got out, went to college and came back in on the flight program," he said. The Air Force has helped him and many others obtain more schooling over the years.

Captain Latham flew more than 300 combat missions in Viet Nam before he was shot down. He was a prisoner of war for about five months. His back and both legs were broken after he parachuted from his damaged jet fighter.

"When the North Vietnamese started releasing pilots in 1973 I got to come home," he said. "The Air Force had a program which allowed pilots to get back into flying. I took it," said Captain Latham.

"While I was a POW, the Thunderbirds were using a 'missing man' formation—a regular formation with one plane missing—to remind their crowds of the men in prison. I think that helped us to get home earlier."

Three Thunderbird officers and a number of the non-commissioned officers (NCOs) stay home most of the time. "While we're out getting the glory they're home doing the work," said one Thunderbird.

Captain Bob Biehl was the chief of maintenance in 1979. He worked between Major Erickson and the enlisted men. "I'm the guy who sees to it the aircraft are ready to fly," he said. "I also have to make sure we have enough of the right supplies.

"If the crew chiefs have a problem they can't take care of themselves, they come to me. If they're at a show site and need a part, or maybe even an engine, that they don't have, I'm the first to know."

Most of the repairs which come from write-ups are minor, Captain Biehl said. If a new engine has to be put in or something big must be done to the airframe, "It requires a functional check flight (FCF). It has to be taken up and tested."

Major Erickson usually takes the FCFs, Captain Biehl added.

"An FCF is just a test to make sure the plane will hold up," Major Erickson said. "I fly it gently and simply at first. Then I fly the loops and rolls at speeds that are used in the show.

"If anything isn't working during the FCF I bring the ship back and turn the crews loose. These people seldom have to fix the same thing twice, though."

Captain Jim Eptins is the team's executive officer. He replaced Major Steve Hyle who left the Thunderbirds in June, 1979.

"The executive officer represents me when I'm not at home," said Major Smith. "In one word, he's the manager of the Thunderbirds. If it involves budgets, planning, security, or personnel, he handles it."

And, in 1979, all team publicity went through Captain Jim Jannette, the public affairs officer. All news releases, photos, and brochures used by the team are developed either by him or by people he supervises.

"We get some time off every once in a while," said a pilot. "But the men who stay behind keep moving all the time. Can you imagine doing everything from writing books to helping reporters and photographers do their job?

"Just keeping track of the fuel we burn could keep one person going for a day or two. I think these people are doing the jobs of twice their number."

"The hours can be long," Captain Jannette said. "But there's a job to be done, and the Thunderbird tradition is that the job *does* get done. That's all."

FEELIN' GOOD

"You won't find many grumpy people around here," said a Thunderbird NCO. "We want people who are happy in their jobs. A person in a bad mood sometimes doesn't do his or her job as well as he or she could."

The NCO admitted that everyone has a bad day every once in a while. "When that happens, the person may get help from others if he or she needs it. Maybe we'll go out of our way just to be nice. I know I've come to work in a bad mood a time or two. But by the time I went home I was feeling good."

"It's such a kick to be part of this team," said another crewman. "When everything else has got me down I remind myself I'm a Thunderbird."

"You have to feel good about your job to work the hours we do," added Sergeant Flannery. "Sometimes we have to work all day and through the night to make an engine change or something like that.

"We wear down. But then, we'll go get a cup of coffee and a snack of some kind, sit and talk for a few minutes and come back to the job ready to get it done."

The Thunderbirds—particularly the pilots—don't always go to the doctors. Sometimes the doctors come to the Thunderbirds.

"I don't know of one group that seems to have fewer injuries and illnesses," said a Nellis flight surgeon. "But it figures. Pilots and NCOs both are in top shape. Even with the long hours and the tiresome traveling they stay in shape. This is a group that really wants to do its job."

The doctor said he drops in on the team from time to time and talks to the people. "If they have something wrong, they usually say so," he said.

"We're pretty sensitive to one another too," said Captain Maness. "If one of us is down a little, the others will try to help him back up. We usually do it, too."

Sometimes, however, a pilot will get sick. Flu bugs have hit the Thunderbirds every once in a while, and other illnesses have grounded one or another pilot.

"If the doctor says you don't fly, that's it," said Captain Evans. "He really has the last word."

When a Thunderbird pilot can't do a show, it simply goes on without him. His part of the show is left out. His only job then is to watch the show, if he can, and join in the debriefing.

If, however, Thunderbird Number One gets sick and is grounded, there will be no show. This has not happened often.

"One time I had ear problems," said a Thunderbird wingman. "The doctor grounded me for one show, but I felt good enough to go out and watch. When the three diamond planes taxied out without me I felt like a kid whose mom and dad had just run off and left him."

But when you're feeling good, "It's really great," said Captain Scarbrough. "It's as though you were part of the aircraft. Your mind works so quickly that you seem to be doing the show in slow motion."

AMBASSADORS IN BLUE

"We represent the Air Force," said a Thunderbird. "We are expected to meet the people wherever we go." At any show site, members of the team are interviewed by reporters. Others may visit schools.

"We always try to help the Air Force recruiters," another member of the team added. "The armed forces now are made up of volunteers. It's important to keep people coming into them."

"In 26 years, Thunderbird pilots and NCOs have spoken to almost every kind of group you could think of," said Captain Jannette. "One of the things we ask our sponsors to do is to line up personal appearances."

"Some of these stops are tiresome, but others are very important to me," said a pilot. "I don't turn down any appearances, really. But I am happiest when I'm visiting in a military or veterans' hospital.

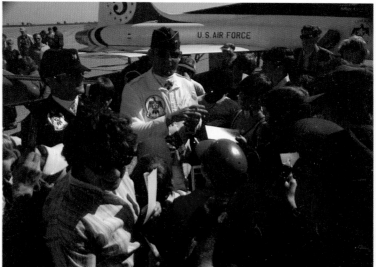

"The people in these hospitals, many of them, were the people who stood behind me when I was in combat. I was luckier than they were. I came out in one piece. I owe something to those in the hospitals."

The Thunderbirds have traveled around the world. Their first trip outside the United States came in 1954. They went to Central and South America. Five years later they flew 30 shows in the Far East, and in 1963 they flew in Europe.

"Almost every year we fly at a couple of sites in Canada," said Captain Jannette. "Just as the Snowbirds (the Canadian Forces team) come to the United States."

Once each year, the Thunderbirds and the Blue Angels of the Navy get together. One year, their meeting will be at Nellis Air Force Base; the next, it's at Sherman Field in Pensacola, Florida.

"We really gear up for the show the Blues will see," said a pilot. "We watch each other closely. The Blues are the only team we can compare ourselves to. When we're flying and they're watching, we try harder."

The Thunderbirds-Blue Angels reunion also is a happy time. Pilots and crews get together for parties and gifts are exchanged. Photographs of the groups are exchanged too.

"We have a lot in common with the Blues," said a pilot. "There are many differences too. The best part of reunion time for me is knowing that there's another group of people doing what we're doing. It's almost a feeling of brotherhood."

The Thunderbirds also welcome hundreds of visitors every year at their "perch" at Nellis Air Force Base.

F-84G

The Thunderbirds have always flown jet aircraft. Their
first plane was the F-84G "Thunderjet," a plane which saw
service in Korea. Their next aircraft, in 1955, was the
F-84F "Thunderstreak."

The two planes were different only because the
"Thunderstreak" had swept-back wings.

F-100

"A change to a new aircraft puts strain on everyone," said a Thunderbird NCO. "The new aircraft usually come in when the training season begins. While the pilots are getting used to flying them, the NCOs have to quickly learn how to maintain them."

The Thunderbirds got their first supersonic plane, the F-100 "Super Sabre," in 1956, then moved on to the F-4E "Phantom" in 1969. Then came the energy crisis of 1974. The Phantom, a real fuel burner, had to go.

"All the Thunderbirds worked their feathers off in '74 to switch the team from the Phantom to the T-38A 'Talon.' The Talon is a much smaller and more economical aircraft," said a Thunderbird. "The season was shortened because of the switch. We still flew 35 shows for two million people."

Thousands of Air Force jet pilots have been trained in Talons, a supersonic trainer. It's one of the smallest jets flown by the Air Force.

"It's a very light aircraft. It is simply built and it's much easier to maintain than some of the larger planes," said Captain Biehl. "Only a few changes have to be made for one of these planes to become a Thunderbird."

"It may be simple," said Captain Scarbrough, "but it's a good plane, too. The Talon can climb at 10,000 feet per minute."

The underside of each Talon is painted with a thunderbird design. This was taken from Indian drawings of the thunderbird, one of the gods of the southwestern Indians.

ABOUT THE AUTHOR

Peter B. Mohn has been following the Performers in Uniform since 1971, but it took five years before he thought about writing about them. When not writing books about flight and flying, he fishes the salt waters around Fort Myers, Florida. He's lived there ever since being cured of Minnesota by the winter of 1977.

INDEX